The Complete

Control Your Money

A quick and easy guide with worksheets

New Readers Press

Acknowledgments
Control Your Money was developed with Lynn Gerrity Ames, CCCC, Vice President, and Eileen D. Muhlig, Director of Education and Public Relations, Consumer Credit Counseling Service of Central New York, Inc.

Thanks to the following people for their contribution to the content of *Control Your Money:* Harold P. Goldberg, Attorney at Law, Syracuse, NY; James Gourley, Pennsylvania New Reader Representative; John Zickefoose, Read Now, Corona Public Library, Corona, CA; and Joanna Miller, Education Coordinator, Southerners for Economic Justice, Durham, NC.

The Complete Control Your Money
ISBN 978-1-56420-275-8

Printed in the United States of America
20 19 18 17 16 15

Proceeds from the sale of New Readers Press materials support professional development, training, and technical assistance programs of ProLiteracy that benefit local literacy programs in the U.S. and around the globe.

Director of Acquisitions and Development: Christina Jagger
Content Editor: Judi Lauber
Copy Editor: Terrie Lipke
Production Director: Deborah Christiansen
Designer: Kimbrly Koennecke
Cover Designer: Kimbrly Koennecke
Illustrator: Linda Tiff
Production Specialist: Shelagh Clancy

Contents

Are You in Control?

Do you control your money, or does your money control you? To find out, try this self-test. Skip any questions that don't apply to you.

True   **False**

____   ____   **1.** I know what my income will be, whether or not it's regular.

____   ____   **2.** I can pay for everything I really need.

____   ____   **3.** I rarely worry about money.

____   ____   **4.** I know how I spent my last paycheck.

____   ____   **5.** I know about how much each monthly bill will be.

____   ____   **6.** I know about how much each yearly or semiyearly bill will be and when I have to pay it.

____   ____   **7.** I rarely have unexpected bills or expenses.

____   ____   **8.** I pay my bills on time.

____   ____   **9.** I have a spending plan and stick to it.

____   ____   **10.** I shop around for sales and good buys.

____   ____   **11.** I balance my checking account each month.

____   ____   **12.** I keep a file of pay stubs, bank statements, receipts, and other financial records.

____   ____   **13.** Without looking, I know about how much cash I'm carrying.

____   ____   **14.** I usually use cash or a check to buy things.

____   ____   **15.** I usually pay the full balance on my credit cards each month.

____   ____   **16.** I don't owe much money, if any.

____   ____   **17.** I save money out of each paycheck.

____   ____   **18.** I have enough insurance, but not too much.

____   ____   **19.** I have a plan to reach my money goals.

If you answered True to most of the questions, you are probably managing your money well. If you answered False to three or more questions, you may want to make some changes.

Chapter 1
Getting Control of Your Money

This book can help you get control of your money. It will give you ideas on how to manage your money well. This can help you reach many of your goals, even if you don't have a lot of money.

First of all, your money should meet your *needs*. These include things you can't do without. They also include payments you must make.

You also use your money for your *wants*. These are things that you could do without. You buy them because you want them.

Your *goals* are things you want in the future. It is easier to stick to a spending plan if you know what goals you are aiming for.

There are two types of goals: short-term and long-term. Short-term goals are things you want to do in the near future.

Long-term goals are the big things that you hope to accomplish someday. It may seem as if long-term goals will never happen. Perhaps some of them won't. But if you plan for them, you can often reach long-term goals more easily than you think.

This chart is a sample list of needs, wants, and goals.

Needs		
	• a place to live • utilities • basic food • basic clothes • transportation	• health care • taxes • repairs • payments on debt • childcare
Wants	• luxury food • luxury clothes • entertainment • hobbies	• magazines • books • computer • cable TV
Short-Term Goals	• buy a car • vacation	• new TV • pay off credit cards
Long-Term Goals	• buy a house • start own business	• send kids to college • retirement income

Short- and Long-Term Goals

Fill in the charts to help plan for meeting your short- and long-term spending goals. If you are not sure how much money you need for a goal, put down your best guess. Divide the amount you need by the number of months before you need the money. This will show how much you need to save each month to meet that goal.

Short-Term Goals (within one year) Examples: • take a vacation • pay off credit cards • buy a TV • buy new shoes for the children	Amount Needed	Months before Needed	Monthly Savings Needed

Long-Term Goals Examples: • buy a new car • pay for children's education • pay for retirement	Amount Needed	Months before Needed	Monthly Savings Needed

Chapter 2
Tracking Your Spending

How do you plan to meet your money needs, wants, and goals? The first step is to set up a spending plan.

Maybe you have tried a spending plan before. If it didn't work out, do you know why?

Perhaps you didn't plan enough for some items or had surprise expenses. Maybe your income was less than you expected. Or maybe you don't know what happened.

☞
> First step in making a spending plan: For four weeks, track your spending. Don't forget small expenses.

A spending plan is a plan for how you will spend your income. You start by tracking what you spend now. Then you decide if you want to make any changes. So the first step is to track your current spending.

For four weeks, write down every penny you spend. You should write down major expenses, such as rent and food. You should also write down minor ones. Include the candy bar you buy, or the money for the parking meter.

☞
> Suppose you put 80¢ in a soda machine every working day. That adds up to almost $200 a year.

The form on page 10 shows one way to track spending. You could use this form, or you could copy it into a small notebook. Then carry it with you. Use it to record everything you spend. (Be sure you carry a pen or pencil too.) That way, you won't forget the small expenses you pay in cash—like tips and snacks. You'll know exactly where all your money is going.

Have everyone in your home track spending. After four weeks, combine the amounts.

It may surprise you to see where your money really goes.

☞

Another way to track spending: Have everyone in the family collect receipts for everything they spend. If you can't get a receipt, make your own—for example: "June 30, Laundromat, $14.75." Collect all the receipts. At the end of each week, have someone sort them into categories and add them up. See page 15 for categories you could use.

Expense Tracking Sheet

Use this form, or one like it, to track your expenses for four weeks. Use more sheets of paper if you need to. Be sure to record every amount you spend, large and small.

	Paid in Cash	Paid by Check	Automatic Payment from Bank Account
Week 1			
Week 2			
Week 3			
Week 4			

Chapter 3

Figuring Your Income and Expenses

Income

☞ Second step in making a spending plan: Figure out your average monthly income.

The next step in making a spending plan is to figure out your income. It's best to figure out average monthly income. That's because many bills are paid monthly.

To figure your income, use take-home pay. This is the amount of money in your paycheck. Income tax, Social Security, and other deductions have usually been taken out already. Take-home pay is the income you can actually spend. Write this information on the form on page 16.

If your pay is regular

If you work, your pay is probably most of your income. But most people aren't paid once a month. How do you figure out monthly pay?

You may get a paycheck that's the same every time. If so, this chart shows how to figure that part of your monthly income:

If you're paid	To find your monthly pay
every week	multiply paycheck by 4
every 2 weeks	multiply paycheck by 2
twice a month	multiply paycheck by 2

If your pay varies

For some people, pay may vary. It could include tips or commissions. The hours people work may vary. Or they may own their own businesses instead of getting a paycheck.

How do you figure out your income if your pay varies? The best way is to figure out average income. Collect all the pay stubs you can find. Add the amounts together. (But don't include overtime pay—you can't always predict when you'll be able to work overtime.) Then divide by the number of pay stubs. This is your average pay per paycheck. Use this amount to find your monthly pay.

What if you have a new job? Or if you expect your pay to change? Try to make your best guess about what will happen in the future. Then see how things go for a few months. Adjust your estimate if necessary.

Other sources of income

You may have other sources of income too:

- child support payments (Note: Be sure you get child support regularly and on time before you count it.)
- disability payments
- pensions
- Social Security
- public assistance or unemployment
- rent from property you own
- gifts or bonuses

Some of these payments might not come once a month. You need to figure all your income in monthly amounts. For each type of payment, figure out how much money you receive in a year and divide it by 12. If the amount varies from year to year, estimate an average amount.

Total household income

Do you share income and expenses with anyone else (for example, a spouse, partner, parent, or child)? In that case, your spending plan should include all the income for your household. Add up everyone's income to get the total household income per month.

The following example shows how to list and figure total monthly income for a household with two people.

Source of Income	Person 1	Person 2
Pay from job	1,200.00	800.00
Other (shoveling snow)	—	130.00
Total	$1,200.00	$930.00
Total for household		**$2,130.00**

Expenses

Third step in making a spending plan: Figure out your average monthly expenses.

Now it is time to list expenses for your spending plan. Try to think of everything you spend money on. Your list should include things you need. You should also list things you don't need but want. The form on pages 16–17 gives you a place to write this information.

Your expenses include
- money you spend
- money you save
- money you invest
- money you give away

For help in making this list, you can look at
- the list you made to track your spending
- your checkbook register
- the list of likely expenses on page 15

Now list the average cost per month for each expense. It's easiest to start with your fixed expenses.

Fixed expenses

Fixed expenses are payments that stay the same. They include such things as rent or mortgage payments, utilities on a budget plan, health insurance, and loan payments.

If you pay a fixed expense every month, write down that amount.

Some expenses are fixed but not paid monthly. Car insurance is an example of this. For these expenses, figure the cost per year. Then divide by 12 to get the monthly cost. That is the amount of money you need to save each month in order to have the payment on hand when you need it. The chart at the top of page 14 shows two examples of figuring fixed expenses.

Item: Car Insurance	Cost: $450 Paid: Twice a year Cost per year = $450 × 2 = $900 Cost per month = $900 ÷ 12 = $75
Item: Vacation Savings Plan	Cost: $15 Paid: Once a week Cost per year = $15 × 52 = $780 Cost per month = $780 ÷ 12 = $65

Variable expenses

Next, look at your variable expenses. These expenses change from month to month. Since the amounts vary, what should you write down?

Some expenses, like groceries, vary a little. For this kind, look up how much you spent in the last three months. Divide this amount by three to get your average monthly cost.

This method won't work for every expense. Some vary too much throughout the year, for example, gifts. Look up how much you spent in the last year. Then divide by 12.

☞

Another way to figure gift expenses: List everyone you buy gifts for. Write down about how much you want to spend on each gift—for birthdays, holidays, and special events. Add to get the yearly total.

Other expenses, like health care, vary a lot from year to year. For such items, add up costs for three years and divide by 36.

This chart gives some examples:

Expense varies	Look up cost for	Divide by	Example	Calculation	Average monthly cost
month to month	last 3 months	3	Groceries—$672 for last 3 months	$672 ÷ 3	$224
within a year	last year	12	Gifts—$540 for last year	$540 ÷ 12	$45
year to year	last 3 years	36	Medical care—$9,684 for last 3 years	$9,684 ÷ 36	$269

Now you have a list of all your average monthly expenses—fixed and variable. The total is the amount you spend per month.

Likely Expenses

Housing
- Rent or mortgage
- Property taxes
- Utilities
  - telephone (including cell phones, beepers)
  - gas & electric
  - water & sewer
  - fuel oil
  - garbage pickup
  - cable TV
- Home maintenance & repairs
- Yard care & snow removal
- Home furnishings & supplies
  - appliances
  - furniture
  - cleaning supplies

Food
- Groceries
- Eating out (including work lunches)

Medical Care (not covered by insurance)
- Medical care
- Eye care
  - glasses
  - contact lenses
- Dental care
- Medicines

Childcare
- Day care & baby-sitting
- Allowances

Transportation
- Gas
- Tolls, parking
- Car maintenance & repairs
- Driver's license & registration
- Public transportation

Clothing
- New clothes
- Laundry & dry cleaning
- Repairs & alterations

Personal
- Cosmetics & toiletries
- Haircuts
- Pet expenses
- Tobacco

Education
- Tuition & fees (including lessons)
- Books
- Room & board

Recreation
- Vacations
- Theater & movie tickets
- Sports events
- Books
- Video rentals
- Newspapers & magazines
- Parties & drinks
- Craft or hobby expenses
- Computer expenses (including Internet)

Gifts & Contributions
- Birthday & holiday gifts
- Religious contributions
- Contributions to charities

Obligations
- Child support
- Car loan or lease payment
- Furniture & appliance loan or rental
- Payments on personal loans
- Credit card payments

Insurance
- Homeowner's or renter's insurance
- Health insurance
- Car insurance
- Disability insurance
- Life insurance

Savings & Investments
- Savings account or CDs
- Savings plans for college & retirement

Income and Expenses

Fill in the charts. Record monthly income and expenses for your household. Use this information to prepare your spending plan. Pages 11–14 have guidelines for finding yearly and monthly totals.

Income	Yearly Total	Monthly Total
Salary/wages (take-home pay)		
Wages from part-time or seasonal jobs		
Income from self-employment		
Other:		
Total Income		

Fixed Expenses	Total for Year (or other period)	Monthly Total
Housing (mortgage or rent)		
Utilities on budget plan		
Property taxes[1]		
Insurance (health, home, car, disability, life)[2]		
Obligations (child support, car loan, etc.)		
Savings and investments (for emergencies, goals, etc.)		
Day care		
Education (tuition, room and board, etc.)		
Other:		
Total Fixed Expenses		

1. If property taxes are part of your mortgage payment, don't list them here too.
2. If any insurance premiums are deducted from your paycheck, don't list them here too.

Variable Expenses	Monthly Total
Utilities (not on budget plan)	
Telephone (including cell phone and beeper costs)	
Home maintenance and repairs	
Yard care and snow removal	
Home furnishings and supplies (appliances, cleaning supplies, etc.)	
Food (groceries; eating out, including work lunches)	
Medical and dental care (not covered by insurance)	
Eye care (glasses, contact lenses)	
Medicines	
Baby-sitting	
Car expenses (gas, tolls, parking)	
Car maintenance and repairs	
Driver's license and car registration	
Transportation other than car	
Clothing (including cleaning and repairs)	
Personal expenses (haircuts, pet expenses, etc.)	
Vacations	
Recreation (movies, sports, videos, computer use, etc.)	
Gifts and contributions (religious institution, charity, etc.)	
Other:	
Total Variable Expenses	

Chapter 4
Making Your Spending Plan Balance

☞ Final step in making a spending plan: Balance the spending plan. Then adjust it to meet your needs, wants, and goals.

Now that you've listed income and expenses, you're done collecting information. Look at your average monthly income and expenses. Are the amounts close?

You want your income and spending to be close. But they will not often match exactly. It's hard to predict income and expenses exactly. The point of a spending plan is to be sure the two don't differ a lot.

Your spending plan now lists your income and expenses from the past. Now you want to turn it into a plan for the future. The first step is to balance the plan.

If Your Spending Plan Doesn't Balance

If your total expenses closely match your income, your spending plan already balances. But if the two sums don't match, you'll need to work to balance it. Use the form on page 19 to check your own income and expenses.

What if your income is larger than your expenses? You could have extra money. You could save or invest more money. Or you could increase the amount you spend on some things.

But maybe you forgot to include some expenses. Search your records and your memory to see if this happened.

If your total expenses are larger than your income, you have two choices. You can cut your spending. Or you can increase your income.

☞ Are you in debt? Having trouble balancing your spending plan? You'll find more information in Chapter 12, page 62.

Does Your Spending Plan Balance?

This form can help you check whether your spending plan balances. An example is done for you. Then use your own figures from the activity on pages 16–17. Does your spending plan balance?

	Example	Your Figures
Total Fixed Expenses	$1,209.32	
Total Variable Expenses	$525.35	
Total Monthly Income	$1,754.21	

Example: Does the spending plan in the example balance?

	Total fixed expenses	$1,209.32
+	Total variable expenses	+ 525.35
=	Total monthly expenses	= $1,734.67

	Total monthly income	$1,754.21
−	Total monthly expenses	− 1,734.67
=	Total monthly balance	= $19.54

Yes, the plan balances. The difference between monthly income and expenses—$19.54—is very small.

Your figures: Does your spending plan balance?

	Total fixed expenses	_____
+	Total variable expenses	+ _____
=	Total monthly expenses	= _____

	Total monthly income	_____
−	Total monthly expenses	− _____
=	Total monthly balance	= _____

Cutting Expenses

If you decide to cut spending, it is easier to cut variable expenses. It is also easier to cut things you want rather than things you need. For example, it is easier to spend less on clothing than to cut down on rent.

But if you have big cuts to make, you may want to cut fixed expenses. You could move into a less expensive apartment. If your area has public transportation, you could sell your car and start riding the bus. Chapters 5 and 12 have more hints on cutting expenses.

Increasing Income

Suppose you decide to increase your income. Here are some possible approaches:

- Look at your payroll deductions. Are you having too much money taken out? (Check with an expert.)
- Find a higher-paying job.
- Take a second job.
- Work more overtime if possible.
- Start your own business on the side.
- If you own rental property, increase the rent if possible.

Adjusting Your Spending Plan

Once your spending plan is balanced, look at it carefully. Would you like to spend less on some things? More on other things? Are you saving as much as you need? This is a good time to think about your goals. Are you saving enough to reach them?

There are no right or wrong answers here. You adjust your spending plan to match your needs, wants, and goals.

Here are some examples of adjustments:

• You want to buy a house in five years. You will need $3,000 for closing costs. You need to save $50 more a month. You cut back on eating out.

• You're self-employed, and you want health insurance. You can get into a group plan through the Chamber of Commerce. The cost is $200 a month. You cut your variable expenses, but it's not enough. You move to a less expensive apartment.

• You spend nearly $10 a week on snacks at work. You decide this is too much. You start bringing snacks from home. You put the extra money in a savings account.

Saving Money for Bigger Expenses

Now you know how much each item in your spending plan costs. You can put money aside from each paycheck for your expenses.

You save a little each month. When a large bill comes due, you won't have to take that amount out of one paycheck.

But where should you keep the money for different expenses? If you lump it all together, it will be hard to keep track of. The system shown below might work for you. Where you keep the money for an expense depends on how often you need to pay that expense.

How Often	Pay By	Keep Money In
every day or every week	cash	budget envelopes. Use one envelope for each item.
every few weeks or every month	check	checking account
every few months or every year	check	savings account (so the money will earn a little interest). Transfer money to checking account when expense is due.

You might want a savings account for long-term goals and another for short-term goals. Be sure you understand the costs before opening more than one account. Many banks charge high fees unless you keep a lot of money in an account. (Chapter 8, page 42, is about savings accounts.)

Here's one way to save for more than one goal in a single account. Suppose George has $800 in his savings account. He knows he needs to pay for car insurance in November. He also wants to save $2,500 for emergencies. He decides he can save $100 out of each paycheck.

This chart shows how George could keep track of the money. At first he splits the $100 between the two goals. Later, when he has enough money for insurance, he puts more money toward his emergency fund.

Goals: Amount needed: Date needed:		Emergency fund $2,500 ASAP	Car insurance $1,020 Nov. 2000
Date	Deposit	for emerg. fund	for car insurance
		$0	$800
7/15/00	$100	+ $75 $75	+ $25 $825
7/31/00	$100	+ $75 $150	+ $25 $850
8/15/00	$100	+ $75 $225	+ $25 $875
8/31/00	$100	+ $75 $300	+ $25 $900
9/15/00	$100	+ $75 $375	+ $25 $925
9/30/00	$100	+ $75 $450	+ $25 $950
10/15/00	$100	+ $75 $525	+ $25 $975
10/31/00	$100	+ $75 $600	+ $25 $1,000
11/15/00	$100	+ $75 $675	+ $25 $1,025
11/30/00	$100	+$100 $775	
12/15/00	$100	+$100 $875	
12/31/00	$100	+$100 $975	

Keeping Track of Savings

You can use this chart to help you keep track of the money in your savings account.

		Goal 1	Goal 2	Goal 3
Goals: Amount needed: Date needed:				
Date	Deposit			
		+ _____	+ _____	+ _____
		+ _____	+ _____	+ _____
		+ _____	+ _____	+ _____
		+ _____	+ _____	+ _____
		+ _____	+ _____	+ _____
		+ _____	+ _____	+ _____
		+ _____	+ _____	+ _____
		+ _____	+ _____	+ _____
		+ _____	+ _____	+ _____
		+ _____	+ _____	+ _____
		+ _____	+ _____	+ _____
		+ _____	+ _____	+ _____
		+ _____	+ _____	+ _____

Chapter 5
Making Money Decisions

There are lots of little ways to save money. Here are some ideas. Pages 26–27 give you a place to write your own ideas.

Smart Shopping

- Do your homework before making a major purchase. Find out as much as you can about different brands and models. Read consumer magazines. Talk to friends.
- Shop around. Find out how much an item costs at different stores in your area.
- Think about service. Some items, such as TVs and computers, may need service. Which stores offer the best service? That might be worth paying a little extra for.
- Buy items on sale when you can.
- Shop at yard sales if you can.
- Buy at the cheapest time. Prices of some products rise and fall according to the season. Try to buy major items when the prices are lowest. This chart shows the best times to buy certain items.

For the best deals on	Try shopping in
appliances	January
lumber, building materials	June
new cars	August, September
used cars	February, November, December
Christmas gifts	January–October
linens	January, May
school clothes and supplies	August, October
tires	May, end of August
air conditioners	February, July, August
TVs	May, June

- Buy quality if you need something to last. Something that is made well will last longer.
- Don't pay for more quality than you need. For example, if your toddler needs shoes, the higher-priced ones might last longer. But she'll outgrow them in a few months.
- Consider buying in quantity if the price per item is lower. But don't buy more than you can store.

- Don't buy more than you can use. You waste money if the item goes bad.
- Use a list when you shop. Stores display small items that people buy on impulse. Don't buy them unless you need them.
- Use coupons—but only if you planned to buy the item anyway.
- Buy store brands instead of name brands.
- Buy produce in season—it costs less.
- Don't let ads convince you to spend more than you planned to. Ask yourself if you really need the product or service.

Eliminate "Extras"

- Check your phone bill. Are you paying for extra services you never use or could do without?
- Check your cable bill. Are you paying for channels you never watch?
- Carry a brown bag lunch to work instead of eating out. It may be only a few dollars—but you'll be surprised at how quickly it can add up.

Create a personal plan for cutting expenses. In each category, list things you can do to reduce your monthly expenses. Put a check next to things you do already.

Food
(Examples: take a bag lunch to work; buy store-brand groceries)

_____

_____

_____

Utilities
(Examples: turn thermostat down at night and while at work;
make long-distance calls when the rates are lower)

_____

_____

_____

Transportation/Car
(Examples: walk whenever possible; learn to do basic car repairs)

_____

_____

_____

Clothing
(Example: wait for seasonal sales)

_____

_____

_____

House Furnishings and Maintenance
(Examples: learn to do basic home repairs, plumbing, etc.;
refinish furniture instead of replacing it)

_____

_____

_____

Recreation
(Examples: rent videos instead of going to the movies; go to a
community-run exercise program instead of a health club)

_____

_____

_____

Personal Expenses
(Examples: get a haircut at a local hairdressing school; give homemade
gifts; look for future gifts when items are on sale)

_____

_____

_____

Other Ideas
(Examples: get books from the library instead of buying them; exchange
favors—baby-sitting, repairs, etc.—with friends or relatives; buy
children's toys at garage sales, secondhand stores, and flea markets)

_____

_____

_____

_____

Saving Money on Energy

- Turn down the heat or air conditioning at night and when you're not home.
- Combine shopping trips.
- Take shorter showers.
- Do some laundry in cold water.
- Put plastic on windows to keep heat in.
- Use old rugs and towels to seal cracks under doors.
- Get a special insulating blanket for your hot-water heater.
- Wrap your hot water pipes with special insulating material.
- Turn down the temperature on your hot-water heater.
- If your water heater is electric, turn it off when you don't need hot water (for example, during the day, when no one is home).

Should You Buy a Home?

For many people, a home is the biggest purchase they ever make. Is buying a home right for you? Here are some pros and cons to consider:

Buying a Home	
Pros	**Cons**
• You control your home. You can redecorate, make improvements, or rent it out.	• You need money for a down payment and closing costs.
• Owning property can be an investment. If you move, you may be able to sell for a profit.	• You probably need to take out a mortgage. This debt usually lasts 15 to 30 years.
• You can deduct property taxes and mortgage interest on your income tax return.	• You have to maintain the home and make repairs. If you have a yard, you need to maintain that, too.
• No one can increase your rent.	• You have to pay for utilities separately.
• You probably get more space for less money than if you rent.	• If you need to move, you might have to sell at a loss.
	• Your property taxes could go up.

☛ Chapter 11, page 55, has more information on home buying.

Tips on Buying a Car

A car is a major purchase. These tips may be helpful.

- If you need a car loan, shop around for it. Credit unions and banks often offer better financing than a dealer. If possible, line up your loan before you start looking at cars.
- If you have an old car, try to sell it yourself. You'll probably get a better deal than if you trade it in.
- Decide if you want a new or used car. A used car may be cheaper. But you could spend more on repairs. A new car may be more reliable and have a warranty. But your payments will be higher.
- Decide what features you want. Don't pay for extras you don't need.
- Check out the model you're interested in. Do you know anyone who owns that type of car? What do consumer magazines say? How reliable is it? On average, how many repairs does it need? How safe is it in accidents? What kind of mileage does it get? How much will the insurance cost?
- Find out where you can get the car serviced. Is it convenient?
- Shop around. How much can you afford to spend? How much are you willing to pay for the car you want? Make your best offer to as many dealers as possible.
- Test drive any car you might buy. Drive it on different types of roads. Get a good feel for how it handles.
- Have the car dealer put the deal in writing. Make sure it includes the price and any promises the dealer made.
- Don't discuss loans or trade-ins with the dealer until you've agreed on a price.

Car Leasing

Are you thinking about leasing a car? Consider carefully before you decide. Lease agreements are complicated, and there can be hidden costs. And at the end of the lease, you won't own the car. The activity on page 30 can help you look at the total cost of leasing.

You may decide leasing is the best deal for you. But make sure you consider all the costs—not just the monthly payment.

☛

When you think about leasing costs, be sure you understand what you'll owe if you return the car early—or if it's totaled in an accident. The costs can be very high.

Is Car Leasing for You?

Fill out this chart to look at the total cost of a car lease.

Due up front:

Security deposit $ _____

Down payment   + _____

First and last lease payments   + _____

Sales tax   + _____

Fees (registration, title, license)   + _____

LESS trade-in[1]   − _____

Total up-front cost $ _____

Paid over time:

Lease payment $_____/month × _____ months = $ _____

Insurance premium[2] $_____/year × _____ years =   + _____

Maintenance costs (provided by dealer)   + _____

Total cost over time   + _____

Due at end of lease:

Charges for excess mileage[3] $ _____

Charges for excess wear and tear[4]   + _____

Final disposition charges   + _____

Balloon payment[5]   + _____

LESS returned security deposit   − _____

Total end-of-lease cost   + _____

Total cost of lease $ _____

1. If you trade in your old car, be sure the amount of the trade-in is written clearly into the lease.
2. A lease will tell you how much insurance you must buy. Make sure you include that cost in your plans.
3. Most leases let you drive 15,000 miles a year. If you drive more, the dealer could charge 8¢ to 15¢ per mile over the limit.
4. At the end of the lease, you'll have to pay for unreasonable wear and tear. Before you agree to a lease, the dealer must tell you how much wear and tear is reasonable.
5. With an "open-end" lease, the car must be worth a certain amount when you return it. That amount is spelled out in the lease. If it's worth less, you have to pay the difference—called a "balloon payment." If you choose a "closed-end" lease, you will not have a balloon payment. But the monthly payments will probably be higher.

Chapter 6
Checking Accounts

A checking account is a place to put money that you don't expect to have long. You pay your bills with that money by writing checks.

A check is an order you write for payment. The bank or credit union takes the money from your account when your check is presented.

How to Write a Check

Payee: The person or company you are paying. You can make out a check to yourself. You can also make it out to "Cash," but that's risky. The bank will cash it for anyone. If it's stolen, you could lose your money.

Date: The day you write a check. A bank may refuse to pay a check that is more than six months old.

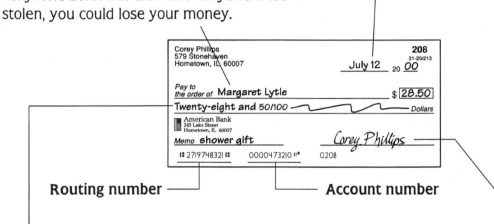

Routing number — Account number

Amount: The amount to be paid. You write this in both words and numbers. If the words and numbers don't agree, the bank may use the amount written in words. Or it may return the check for you to correct. If someone else changes the amount, the bank should not cash the check. If it does, it must refund your money.

Signature: Your signature approves the payment. If someone else signs your name to a check, it is a forgery. You are usually not responsible if the bank cashes a forged check. You can ask the bank to refund your money.

How to Cash a Check

Before cashing a check, sign your name on the back. Your signature must appear within 1½ inches of the end. You can also write "for deposit only" and your account number above your signature. This insures that the money goes into your account. See the example below.

Choosing a Checking Account

There are different types of checking accounts. One bank or credit union may offer several kinds.

- Some accounts are free. There is no service fee. But it's not easy to find a free checking account.
- For some accounts, the bank charges a service fee by the month, by the check, or both.
- Some accounts are free if you keep a minimum balance. This amount is at least a few hundred dollars.
- Some accounts pay you interest on your money. The interest rate is often low.
- Some banks reduce or drop fees if you have direct deposit.

When you want to open a checking account, find out what types are offered by local banks and credit unions. Look at these features:

- **Fees.** How much will the account cost you?
- **Restrictions.** What restrictions apply to the account? Is there a minimum balance? A limit on how many checks you can write? How soon can you use money after you deposit it?
- **Location.** Is the bank near your home or work?
- **Convenience.** What hours is the bank open? Will you be able to get there during its business hours?
- **Other services.** Does the bank offer services you are interested in? Overdraft protection? Credit cards? Debit cards? Pay-by-phone service?

The activity on page 34 lets you compare costs and services of different checking accounts.

Once you choose a bank and open a checking account, you will have to buy your checks. You can buy them through the bank. You can also get checks from other sources, for example, printing companies. Checks from printing companies often cost less. But you have to inspect the checks carefully. Make sure all the information—including account numbers and routing numbers—are correct.

If you share expenses with someone else, you may want to open a joint account. The account will have both names on it. Either of you can make deposits, write checks, and make withdrawals. But a joint checking account can be a lot of work. You both have to keep careful records of deposits, withdrawals, and checks you write. And you have to tell each other promptly. If your communication is unclear, you could wind up spending money that you don't have.

Term	What It Is	Pros and Cons
Direct deposit	A payment (for example, your paycheck or Social Security check) is put directly into your checking account. You don't have to deposit it.	• Makes your money available sooner. • Is convenient and safe. • Can be helpful if you have trouble getting to the bank.
Overdraft protection	Even if you don't have enough money in your account, the bank pays your checks. It charges you interest until you pay the money back.	• Tends to be very costly, with high interest rates and fees. • May make it tempting to overspend.
Debit card	You get a card that looks like a credit card. But when you use it, the payment comes out of your bank account right away. (Sometimes called a "check card.")	• Saves trouble of writing checks. • Can be used wherever you can use a credit card. • Requires careful record keeping so you don't overdraw your account.
Automatic withdrawal	At your request, the bank automatically pays a regular bill (such as a loan payment).	• Saves the trouble of writing a monthly check. • Makes sure your payment is on time. • You need to be sure you have enough money in your account. • To cancel, you have to tell the bank in writing.
Pay-by-phone service	You can pay bills by calling the bank. You tell the bank how much to send for each bill.	• Saves the trouble of writing a check. • You need to have enough money in your account.

The Real Cost of Checking

Compare the costs of checking accounts at different banks or credit unions. Fill in the information for two different ones. If you have a checking account, fill in the information for your account and one other. Use this information to find a good deal on checking.

Fees and Benefits	Choice 1	Choice 2
Name of bank or credit union		
1. Monthly maintenance fee		
2. 2a. Fee for each check written		
2b. Number of checks I write each month: ____		
Monthly check-writing cost (2a × 2b)		
3. Bounced check fee		
4. 4a. Fee for using the bank's ATM		
4b. Fee for using other ATMs		
4c. Number of times I use an ATM each month: ____		
Estimated monthly ATM costs (based on 4a, 4b, and 4c)		
5. 5a. Fee for using teller service		
5b. Number of times I use teller service each month: ____		
Monthly cost of teller service (5a × 5b)		
6. Minimum balance for free checking		
7. Free checking with direct deposit?	❏ yes ❏ no	❏ yes ❏ no
8. Interest bank will pay on account balance		
9. Overdraft protection?	❏ yes ❏ no	❏ yes ❏ no
10. Interest I will pay on overdrafts		
11. Other fees: _____		
_____		
12. Other benefits: _____		
_____		

Paying by Check

In many cases it is better to pay bills with a check than with cash. Paying by check is safer when you pay through the mail. It is not safe to send cash through the mail.

You may also want to pay large bills by check, even if you pay in person. You may not feel safe carrying a large amount of cash.

The payee cashes your check at the bank. The bank takes the money out of your account. Many banks then mail the check back to you. A check that has been paid is called a canceled check. You can use the canceled check to prove you paid.

Some banks don't send checks back to you. Instead they send a list of the checks they have paid from your account. If you need a check as proof of payment, the bank will send you a copy. Some banks charge you for this service.

Each checkbook has a place to record the checks you write:

- a separate register,
- check stubs, or
- a carbon copy of each check.

You use this place to record the payee, the date, and the amount of each check.

You should also use your record of checks to keep track of how much money is in your account. This is called your balance.

Stopping Payment

What if you decide you don't want the bank to pay a check you wrote? Or you lose a check? You can give the bank a stop payment order. You can do this on the phone or in person. The bank will charge you a fee to stop payment.

It's important to make the stop payment order as soon as you find a problem. You have to contact the bank before the check is paid. If you wait too long, you could lose your money.

Bouncing a Check

A check bounces if you don't have enough money in your account to cover it. Many people bounce checks because they make a mistake. Sometimes the bank makes a mistake that causes a check to bounce. (Note: Bouncing a check on purpose is a crime.)

These things can cause checks to bounce:

- You don't keep track of how much money is in your account.
- You keep track, but you make a mistake in doing the math.
- A deposit doesn't clear before checks are presented against it.

Federal rules set how quickly banks must clear deposits. Some deposits are available the next day. Some can take up to five days. If you make your deposit at an ATM, it may take longer.

If it's your mistake, bouncing a check can be costly. The bank will charge you a bounced check fee. The payee may also charge you.

To avoid bounced checks, keep careful track of how much money is in your account. Subtract your checks as you write them. Wait for a deposit to clear before you write checks against it.

If the bank makes a mistake, it won't charge you a bounced check fee. It must also explain to the payee that the problem wasn't your fault. Ask the bank to write a letter of explanation. And be sure you keep a copy of it.

ATMs

An ATM (automated teller machine) card is a plastic card with a magnetic stripe on the back. With it, you can withdraw cash from your account. You can also perform other transactions. Banks provide ATM cards with most checking accounts. Some banks charge a fee for these cards.

You can use an ATM at your bank. You can also use other ATMs, if they are part of the same network. Your bank may charge you a fee every time you use an ATM. There may be no fee if you use an ATM at your own bank. But you may be charged if you go elsewhere.

A PIN is a secret number. If you have a choice, pick a random number. Don't use your birthday, address, or phone number. And never write your PIN on your card or in your checkbook. It's not a good idea to tell anyone your PIN, either. With your ATM card and your PIN, anyone can get money out of your account.

To use an ATM:
1. Insert your ATM card. The screen display asks for your personal identification number (PIN).
2. Enter your PIN. The screen asks what you want to do.
3. Choose the transaction you want. You can usually choose
   - withdrawing cash from your checking or savings account
   - depositing checks into your checking or savings account
   - transferring money between accounts
   - checking your account balance or your credit card balance
   - some other transactions
4. When you finish your transactions, the ATM returns your card. It may give you a receipt or ask if you want one. Keep the receipt to check against your bank statement. Be sure to record the transactions in your checkbook or savings account records, too.

credit card balance: the total amount owed on a credit card

account balance: the amount of money in a bank account

Money Orders

If you don't have a checking account, money orders may be an option. You can buy money orders at banks, post offices, and other places. They can be useful. But they have drawbacks:
- You have no record of when the money order is cashed. This means you can't prove that you made the payment.
- You can't stop payment once you send a money order.
- The amount of a money order is limited. Ask the seller the limit.

If you'll be paying many bills, a checking account is probably a better option.

Match each banking term with its definition.

_____ **1.** canceled check

_____ **2.** PIN

_____ **3.** stop payment order

_____ **4.** automatic withdrawal

_____ **5.** account balance

_____ **6.** overdraft protection

_____ **7.** direct deposit

_____ **8.** service fee

_____ **9.** minimum balance

_____ **10.** interest

a. the amount of money you have in a bank account

b. the amount of money you must have in an account to get a service such as no-fee checking

c. the amount you pay (per check or per month) to have a checking account

d. a check that has been cashed

e. a loan from the bank to cover your checks if you don't have enough money in your account

f. an amount the bank pays you; a percent of the total amount in your account

g. a secret number that identifies you at an ATM

h. money that is taken out of your account without your doing anything; for example, for a loan or a utility payment

i. your command to the bank not to cash a check that you wrote

j. a service that puts money (for example, from an employer or Social Security) into your account automatically

Answers on page 80.

Chapter 7
Balancing Your Checkbook

To keep track of your checking account, you record checks, withdrawals, charges, and deposits. But that isn't enough. When you get a bank statement, you should balance your checkbook. This means making sure you agree with the bank about how much money is in your account.

The bank sends you regular statements about your account. The statement shows the deposits you have made, the checks that have been paid, and the following items:

- service fees
- bills you paid by phone
- fees for bounced checks
- withdrawals you made through an ATM
- automatic withdrawals, such as loan payments or savings club deductions
- payments you made with a debit card (Page 33 includes information about debit cards.)

To balance your checkbook, use the chart on page 40. Use a calculator if you can.

If the two totals match, you are done. Your checkbook is balanced. If not, take these steps:

- Compare each canceled check to the bank statement. Make sure the amounts match. If they don't, you will have to call the bank to correct the problem. If your bank keeps the canceled checks rather than sending them back, you can compare the bank statement to your checkbook.
- Compare the amount of each check to the amount written in your checkbook. If you wrote down the wrong amount, correct it. If you forgot to write down a check, include it now. Adjust your balance.
- Compare deposits against the bank statement. Make sure the amounts match. If they don't, you can use the deposit slip to show the bank how much you deposited.

Balancing a Checkbook

Use this form to help you balance your checkbook.

Step 1

Start with new balance from bank statement. $_____.___

List checks and other withdrawals from your checkbooks not listed on the bank statement:

_____.___
_____.___
_____.___

Total: _____.___

Subtract total from bank statement balance.   −_____.___

List deposits from your checkbook not listed on the bank statement:

_____.___
_____.___
_____.___

Total: _____.___

Add total to bank statement balance.   +_____.___

Adjusted bank statement balance $_____.___

Step 2

Start with balance from your checkbook. $_____.___

List any fees or other deductions on the bank statement not listed in your checkbook.*

_____.___
_____.___
_____.___

Total: _____.___

Subtract total from checkbook balance.   −_____.___

List any interest or other deposits on the bank statement not listed in your checkbook.*

_____.___
_____.___
_____.___

Total: _____.___

Add total to checkbook balance.   +_____.___

Adjusted checkbook balance $_____.___

Do the totals match?

*Be sure to put these amounts in your checkbook register each month after you balance your checkbook.

☞ You should save your deposit slips throughout the month. That way you can check them against the bank statement.

- Compare the withdrawals that appear on the bank statement with those you have written in your checkbook. Be sure you haven't forgotten any withdrawals.

After you've done all this, your checkbook should balance. If it still doesn't, check everything again. Also check for these errors:

- Did you make a math mistake in your checkbook? Use a calculator if you can.
- Check the balance you carried from page to page in your checkbook. Did you write the wrong amount?

If the two totals still don't match, see if a friend can help you. Some nonprofit agencies will also help people straighten out their checking accounts.

☞ Bank statements are usually right. But if you find a bank error, report it as soon as possible. If you don't, you could lose money.

Chapter 8
Savings Accounts

When you save, you make progress toward your money goals. You also set aside money for emergencies.

Experts give these tips on saving money:

- Save something out of each paycheck, even if it's only a little.
- Think of savings as a bill you pay yourself. Pay yourself first.
- If you can, have your savings deducted from your paycheck before you get it.
- Don't save so much money that you don't have enough to live on.
- Once you put money into savings, forget it exists. Don't use it to pay day-to-day bills.

Banks and credit unions offer different kinds of savings accounts. The chart on page 43 gives information on some common types of savings accounts. When you check out a bank, look for signs that say "Member FDIC" or "FDIC Insured." They mean that the bank accounts are insured by the government. You won't lose your money even if the bank fails.

You will probably start saving by putting money in a regular savings account. When you have enough money, you might want to put some savings into CDs (certificates of deposit). They earn more interest. A CD is a type of investment. For more on investing, see Chapter 14, page 72.

You can buy CDs at your bank. A CD is a promise to leave your money on deposit for a certain length of time. The bank pays higher interest on CDs because it can plan on having the money for that amount of time. At the end of that time, the CD matures, and you can withdraw the money. If you cash in a CD early, you'll have to pay a penalty.

You can buy CDs in different amounts. The lowest is usually $500. You can also buy them for different periods of time. CDs with longer terms pay higher interest.

You may decide to buy more than one CD. If so, try to make sure they mature at different times. That way you will always have money available if you need it.

Account Type	Description	Pros	Cons
Regular savings accounts (also called deposit accounts)	• You deposit money whenever you want. • You may have a passbook that shows your balance. Or you may get a regular statement from the bank or credit union.	• Your money earns interest. • You can withdraw your money any time. • Your interest may increase if rates go up. • You may get free checking if you have a savings account.	• CDs and Money Market accounts pay more interest. • You may need to keep a minimum balance. • Your interest may decrease if rates go down.
Savings clubs	• You deposit a fixed amount every week. • The account helps you save for a special purpose: holiday gifts or vacation.	• You can save for big expenses a little at a time.	• Your money may not earn interest.
CDs (certificates of deposit)	• You deposit $500 or more. • You agree to leave the money for a certain period (from a month to 5 years).	• You get higher interest than with regular savings. • Your interest rate stays the same, even if rates go down. • You can use CDs to plan for future money needs.	• Your money is tied up for a specific period. • You pay large penalties if you withdraw it early. • Your interest rate stays the same, even if rates go up.
Money Market accounts	• You deposit a large amount to open the account. • The bank pays you interest based on the money market. • You can write a few checks each month.	• You get higher interest than with regular savings. • Your interest rate can go up.	• You have to keep a large minimum balance. If you don't, the bank charges high fees. • Your interest rate can go down. • These accounts are usually not insured.

Experts suggest that you keep between three and six months' pay in regular savings accounts and CDs. This should be enough for emergencies. If you have more than that, consider other types of investments. Other investments will often pay more interest.

Choosing a Savings Account

Look at your spending plan. How much can you save?

I can deposit $_____ to open an account. Then I will save $_____

every week/month/other: _____.

Now, use this chart to judge how accounts will meet your needs:

	Choice #1	Choice #2	Choice #3
Name of bank or credit union			
Type of account	❏ deposit account ❏ savings club ❏ CD ❏ Money Market	❏ deposit account ❏ savings club ❏ CD ❏ Money Market	❏ deposit account ❏ savings club ❏ CD ❏ Money Market
Can I get to the bank conveniently?	❏ yes ❏ no	❏ yes ❏ no	❏ yes ❏ no
How much money do I need to open an account?			
How much interest does it pay?			
Do I have to keep a minimum balance?	❏ yes ❏ no	❏ yes ❏ no	❏ yes ❏ no
If so, how much?			
Is there a penalty if my balance falls lower?	❏ yes ❏ no	❏ yes ❏ no	❏ yes ❏ no
If so, how much?			
When can I withdraw my money?			
Is there a penalty if I withdraw it early?	❏ yes ❏ no	❏ yes ❏ no	❏ yes ❏ no
If so, how much?			
Is the account insured?	❏ yes ❏ no	❏ yes ❏ no	❏ yes ❏ no

The Complete

Chapter 9
Why Use Credit?

When you use credit, you borrow money. You have to pay back what you borrowed, plus interest. Interest is the cost of using credit.

Common kinds of credit include

- bank loans
- store credit cards
- bank credit cards (such as MasterCard and VISA)
- mortgages

The sooner you pay back the money, the less interest you pay.

☞ Be aware of the difference between credit cards and charge cards. With a credit card, you can pay off your balance over time. You'll pay interest on the balance. With a charge card, you must pay the whole balance when you get the bill. American Express, for example, offers a major charge card.

Before you buy something, decide whether you want to pay now or use credit. The chart below sums up things to consider.

Pay Now: Advantages	Use Credit: Advantages
• You can't spend more money than you have. • You don't have to pay interest. • You can shop anywhere you want. • You don't risk buying something that you may not be able to pay for.	• You can buy and use things now, instead of having to save for them. • You can sometimes buy something on sale and save money, even if you don't have the cash. • You can buy things that most people are never able to save the cash for. A house is a good example.

What if you plan never to borrow money? You still may want to have a credit card. It's often easier to pay by check if you can show a credit card as ID. And it is harder to rent a car without a credit card. Some people use their credit cards only as ID.

☞ ....

Protect your money from thieves: If you use a credit card for ID, don't let anyone write down the number. Also, don't give your credit card number or checking account number to someone who calls you on the phone.

It can also be a good idea to have a credit card for emergencies. What if you didn't have enough cash and

- your car broke down far from home?
- you had to travel to another city for a family emergency?
- you needed cash on a weekend and didn't have an ATM card?

You can use a credit card for all these things.

What if you still don't want a credit card? Or you have trouble getting one? You might want to consider a debit card. A debit card looks and works like a credit card. But the money comes right out of your checking account. You don't get a bill or have to pay interest.

☞ ....

When you use a debit card, the money must already be in your account.

The activity on page 47 lets you explore your own views on cash versus credit.

Cash or Charge?

What are your views on using cash or credit cards? Answer these questions.

1. How do you usually pay for things? Check all that apply.

    _____ Cash   _____ Check   _____ Money order

    _____ Credit card   _____ Charge card   _____ Debit card

    _____ Other

2. Do you use one method more often than others? _____ Yes _____ No

    Which one? _____ Why? _____

    _____

3. What kind of credit cards do you have? Check all that apply.

    _____ Bank card(s)   _____ Store card(s)   _____ Other

4. Are credit cards a good idea for you? _____ Yes _____ No

    Why or why not? _____

    _____

5. What's the best thing about having a credit card? _____

    _____

6. What's the worst thing about having a credit card? _____

    _____

7. What problems could you have if you don't have a credit card? _____

    _____

8. What are some reasons to use cash instead of a credit card? _____

    _____

Chapter 10
Getting Credit

The Three Cs

When you apply for a loan or a credit card, lenders judge whether you will repay your debt. They are concerned about three Cs:
- **Capacity.** Can you repay this loan? How much do you earn? How long have you been at your job? How much do you owe?
- **Character.** Can you be trusted to pay your debts? What is your credit history? Do you pay your bills on time?
- **Collateral.** Do you own property that could back up the loan?

Building a Credit History

It can be hard to get credit for the first time. Since you have no credit history, lenders don't know whether they can depend on you.

Here are some ways to build your credit history:
- Have a steady work record.
- Pay your bills on time.
- Keep your utility bills.
- Keep a checking account. Don't bounce checks.
- Keep a savings account. Make regular deposits.

48   **The Complete**

Once you've done these things, apply for a local store credit card. (This is easier to get than a major credit card.) Use the card a few times. Make sure you pay the bill on time.

You can also apply for a small loan. Use your savings account as collateral. Pay back the loan on time.

Co-Signing Loans

Asking someone to co-sign

You may need a bigger loan for a car or other large purchase. If you have no credit history, you could be turned down.

If this happens, you can ask someone to co-sign the loan. This person should be a relative or close friend with a good credit history. A co-signer promises to pay back the loan if you don't.

☞ Remember, any time you borrow money, make all the payments on time.

Should you co-sign?

If you have a good credit history, someone may ask you to co-sign a loan. Think carefully before you agree. Ask yourself:

- Why does this person need someone to co-sign? (If it is because of a bad credit history, be careful. You could get stuck paying off the loan.)
- Can I afford to make the payments if this person doesn't?
- Will I still be able to get the credit I need if I co-sign for this loan?
- Can I depend on this person? Does this person have a steady income?

If You're Turned Down for Credit

What if you're turned down when you apply for credit?
Anyone who turns you down must

- send you a written denial letter
- give you in writing the reasons you were rejected, or tell you how to request those reasons
- give you the name, address, and telephone number of any credit reporting agency that provided a credit report on you
- tell you what other information was used, if any

Check the information used to be sure it's all correct. If there are mistakes, write to the lender about them.

Credit Reports

Credit reporting agencies collect information from creditors. They find out how much money you owe and if you pay your bills on time. They sell this information to lenders and others who have your permission.

☞

Credit reporting agencies collect information from
- public records
- retail stores
- credit card companies
- banks, mortgage companies, and other lenders
- student loan records

A credit reporting agency may sell information to someone who is thinking of
- lending you money
- giving you a credit card
- selling you life insurance
- hiring you
- renting you an apartment

☞

A credit report costs up to $8. But if you've been turned down for credit or a job in the last 60 days, it is free.

Checking your credit report

You can check your credit report. You can contact the credit reporting agencies listed in Chapter 15, page 78. Or look in the yellow pages under "Credit" or "Credit Reporting." Call each company and ask if it has a file about you. If it does, ask the cost of a report.

To get a credit reporting agency's information about you, send the agency a written request along with your payment. Include

- your full name, and any other names you have used
- your current and most recent previous address, with zip codes
- your spouse's name, if you are married
- your Social Security number
- your year of birth
- your signature

What if you've never been turned down for credit? It's still a good idea to check your credit report once in a while. You can make sure that everything in it is correct.

Reading a credit report

Credit reports from different companies look different. But they all contain the same kind of information:

- **personal information**—your name, address, employer, date of birth, Social Security number, former addresses, former employers
- **public records**—any court records that affect your credit, like bankruptcy, liens on your property, and court judgments against you
- **inquiries**—a list of companies that have requested your credit report in the past two years
- **credit history information**—past and present credit accounts, like credit and charge cards and bank loans

For each credit account, the report lists this kind of information:

- name of the company
- account number
- type of account (for example, individual or joint charge account, secured or unsecured loan)
- "high credit"—the most you've ever owed on the account, or your credit limit
- the last time you used or paid on the account
- how much you owe on the account, and how much of that is past due
- how many times your payments have been late (Most credit reports list how many times you've been 30, 60, and 90 or more days late.)

The activity on page 52 lets you practice reading a sample credit report.

Reading a Credit Report

Look at this sample credit report. Then answer the questions below.

```
CONSUMER IDENTIFICATION
TERRY CROWLEY                                                            DATE 07/03/01
123 MAPLE AVE APT 4              SSN 000-00-0000
SPRINGFIELD, MA 01101           DOB 02/29/64

CREDIT HISTORY
                  ACCT    HIGH      DATE     LAST                PAST    # TIMES PAST DUE
COMPANY   ACCT #  TYPE    CREDIT    REPORTED ACTIVITY   BALANCE  DUE     30    60    90+
VISA      XXXXXX  INDIV   9762      03/01    11/00      245      0
SEARS     XXXXXX  JOINT   5000      02/01    01/01      2732     635     02    03    01
CHASE     XXXXXX  SECURE  11388     02/01    10/99      0        0

PUBLIC RECORDS
BANKRUPTCY FILED 09/97; NORTHERN DIST CT; LIABILITIES-$12851; PERSONAL; INDIVIDUAL;
DISCHARGED; ASSETS-$870

INQUIRIES
JC PENNEY    06/03/01          HOME BANK      05/14/00
MACYS        11/16/00          IMPORT AUTO    03/19/00

PLEASE ADDRESS ANY CORRESPONDENCE REGARDING YOUR CREDIT REPORT TO:  CREDIT REPORTING
                                                                    321 MAIN ST SUITE 17
                                                                    SPRINGFIELD, MA 01101
```

1. What credit accounts does the report show? _____

2. Which account is a secured loan? _____

   Which is an individual account? _____

3. How much does Terry Crowley owe VISA? _____

   What is the most Terry has ever owed VISA? _____

4. Which account is past due? _____

   How much is past due? _____

5. When did Terry Crowley file for bankruptcy? _____

6. How many companies have checked Terry Crowley's
   credit history in the past two years? _____

7. Where should Terry Crowley write with corrections
   or questions about this credit report? _____

   _____

   _____

Answers on page 80.

The Complete

Correcting Your Credit Report

What if you find an error on your credit report? You have the right to dispute it. The checklist on page 54 gives the steps for checking and correcting a credit report.

To ask for a correction, write to the credit reporting agency. Explain the error. You should also write to the company that supplied the wrong information. Be sure to contact each credit reporting agency that has an error in its report.

The credit reporting agency will check your story. If it agrees with you, it will correct the report. If it makes a change, it must give you a free copy of your new credit report.

Check the report in 90 days to be sure the mistake was fixed.

Sometimes the credit reporting agency will not agree with you. If it doesn't, it does not have to change your credit report. But you can make a 100-word consumer comment to explain your side. The credit reporting agency must include your comment in future reports. Tell the agency you want the comment at the beginning of your report.

☞ Example: You bought a VCR on credit. It didn't work. You refused to pay until the store fixed it. Now your credit report says you paid the bill late. You can get your side of the story into the report.

Bad Credit History

You can't erase bad credit history. Most facts stay on your record for seven years. If you go bankrupt, that can stay on your record for 10 years. (Chapter 12, page 62, discusses bankruptcy.) Some companies claim to fix a bad credit history. Don't believe them. Nothing but time can do that.

Credit Checkup Checklist

It's a good idea to check your credit report every year or two. This checklist can help.

_____ 1. Contact the credit reporting agency. Ask how to get a copy of your credit report.

_____ 2. Send a request to the credit reporting agency. Follow the agency's instructions, and send the fee, if needed.

_____ 3. When you receive the report, check it carefully. Look for
  • old information
  • incorrect information
  • missing or incomplete information
  • unauthorized inquiries

_____ 4. If you find any problems, report them to the credit reporting agency. Use the agency's dispute form.

_____ 5. Be specific about why you think information is wrong, for example:
  • The report says you made late payments when you didn't.
  • The report lists information about someone else.
  • The report lists an account that you closed.
  • The report says a debt is unpaid, but you know you paid it.
  • The report lists negative information that is more than 7 years old (10 years old for bankruptcy).

_____ 6. With the dispute form, send *copies* of any evidence that supports you (letters, receipts). Do not send the originals.

_____ 7. When you receive an answer, check to see whether the credit reporting agency agreed to correct your report.

_____ 8. If the credit reporting agency doesn't correct your report, write a letter. Tell your side of the story in 100 words or less. Ask the credit reporting agency to include the statement at the beginning of your credit report.

_____ 9. After a few months, get another copy of your credit report. Check that the credit reporting agency has made any changes it agreed to and has included your written statement, if you made one.

Chapter 11
Credit Cards and Loans

Credit Cards

Suppose you want a credit card. How do you decide which one? Ask yourself, "How am I going to use this card?"

Not all credit cards have the same terms. The differences will affect how much the card costs you. The terms include

- annual percentage rate (APR)
- grace period
- annual fee
- transaction fees

The APR is the interest rate, measured by the year. The APR on major credit cards can vary a lot. On some it is as low as 9 percent. On others it can be as high as 22 percent. Introductory rates may be lower, but usually go up after a stated period.

The grace period is the time you have to pay your bill before you are charged interest. Some credit cards do not have a grace period. That means you owe interest from the moment you charge something.

The annual fee is a yearly charge for having the card. For most cards the fee is between $15 and $50. Some cards have no annual fee.

You pay a transaction fee when you miss a payment, go over your credit limit, or use the card to get cash. Some cards charge a monthly fee whether you use the card or not.

How do you pick the right card for you? Think of how you will use your card. The table below has some suggestions.

How You Use Your Card	Most Important Features
You use your card for ID. You rarely use it to buy anything.	Low or no annual fee No monthly fee
You pay off your whole balance every month.	Long grace period
You carry a balance from month to month.	Low APR

Closing your account

Suppose you have a credit card you never use. It may be a good idea to close the account. Cut the card in half and throw it away. Pay off the balance of your account. Then write to the company and say you want to close the account. Send the letter by certified mail so you can prove the company got your request. Ask the company to send verification that the account is closed.

You may want to close credit card accounts if you find you're charging too much. It will keep you from running up more debt.

Loans

You want to buy something big—perhaps a car or a house. Should you take out a loan? How much will it cost?

Banks, credit unions, and other lenders offer different kinds of loans. This section covers some loan basics, but it doesn't include everything.

If you're thinking of borrowing, it's important to get good advice. Be sure you know what's involved before you sign anything. You may want to consult an expert—a financial planner, credit counselor, or loan officer at a bank.

Loan basics

When you borrow, you agree to pay back the money with interest. Can you afford it? You need to look at these four factors:

- monthly payments
- interest rate
- length of the loan
- fees

Experts say your monthly loan payments should total no more than 10 percent of your monthly take-home pay. (Don't count mortgage payments in this total.)

Find out what the monthly payments will be. Can you afford them?

If you take out a car loan, you have to pay it off, even if the car is stolen or destroyed.

Match each credit term with its definition. Then fill in the information about the terms of your credit card.

_____ 1. grace period

_____ 2. minimum payment

_____ 3. APR

_____ 4. balance

_____ 5. annual fee

_____ 6. transaction fee

_____ 7. interest

_____ 8. credit limit

a. the amount you pay each year for the right to use a credit card

b. the maximum amount you can charge in a billing period

c. the time between the date of a bill and the time you start paying interest on what you owe

d. the extra amount you pay if you pay in installments

e. the smallest part of your bill that you have to pay each month

f. the interest rate calculated for a full year

g. the amount you owe on your bill at a given time

h. the extra amount you pay when you use your card to get cash

Answers on page 80.

Fill in the information for your credit card.

annual fee: _____

transaction fee: _____

credit limit: _____

APR: _____

minimum payment: _____

The lower the interest rate, the cheaper the loan—all other things being equal. Some loans have variable interest rates. The starting rate is usually lower than on fixed rate loans. But your payments can get higher over time.

A loan with a shorter term will have higher monthly payments. But the total will be less. This table shows the costs of two loans for the same amount at the same interest. The longer loan costs almost $2,000 more.

Loan Amount	Interest Rate	Term	Monthly Payment	Total Paid
$13,500	12.5%	3 years	$451.62	$16,258.32
$13,500	12.5%	5 years	$303.72	$18,223.20

Most lenders charge fees as well as interest. Fees can quickly increase a loan's cost. Some lenders charge a penalty if you pay off a loan early.

By law, a lender must give you a Truth-in-Lending Disclosure Statement. This statement shows how much you're borrowing. It also shows how much you must repay—including interest and fees. See the chart on page 59 for a way to compare loan terms.

☞ A Truth-in-Lending Disclosure Statement is the only document that spells out the total cost of a loan.

Mortgages

Most people need to borrow if they buy a home. This kind of loan is a mortgage. In general, mortgages have terms of 15 to 30 years.

Your monthly mortgage payment includes the loan payment (principal and interest), property taxes, and homeowner's insurance. It may also include private mortgage insurance.

☞ Some lenders will "prequalify" you for a mortgage. They will take some basic financial information. They will then tell you how big a mortgage they think you can afford. This saves you the trouble and expense of applying for a mortgage that's too big for you. But be sure you agree that you can afford the monthly payments, as well as upkeep on the home.

The Complete

Getting the Facts on a Loan

Before you sign a loan contract, be sure you understand all its terms. Use this form to compare some important items. If you can't find this information in the loan papers, ask. The law requires a lender to tell you these things.

	Lender 1	Lender 2	Lender 3
Company making the loan			
Amount of the loan			
Charges covered by payments (taxes, fees, interest, etc.)			
Any annual fees			
Finance charge in dollars and as an annual percentage rate (APR)			
Amount of each payment			
When each payment is due, and the grace period, if any			
Fees for late payments			
Total amount you will pay			

You pick a mortgage lender once you've

- found a home you want
- agreed on a price
- signed a purchase agreement to buy the home
- paid a deposit

To find out about mortgage lenders, check ads in the newspaper real estate section. You can also ask friends and coworkers or your lawyer. Find out which lenders they think are good.

☞ --

Experts say you should always have a lawyer when you buy a home.

Nonprofit agencies that do housing counseling can also help you find out about lenders. And they can tell you if you qualify for any special mortgage programs.

Certain special mortgage programs help low- and moderate-income home buyers:

- Veterans Administration (VA) mortgages help veterans to buy houses. Down payments are often very low.
- With Federal Housing Administration (FHA) mortgages, you may need only a 3 to 5 percent down payment.
- Rural Housing Service (RHS) loans help people buy homes in rural areas. If you qualify, you may not need a down payment.
- Other national mortgage programs also offer options for lower down payments and closing costs. And they may have more flexible income requirements. The corporations Fannie Mae and Freddie Mac offer such options.
- In addition, many state programs give first-time home buyers a lower interest rate.

Suppose you've found a mortgage lender. The next step is to fill out a mortgage application. On this form, you supply detailed financial information. You pay application costs—usually several hundred dollars. (Note: You won't get this money back, even if you don't get the mortgage.)

It may take a few weeks for the lender to process your application. If the lender approves you for the mortgage, you'll get a commitment letter. The letter tells

- how much money you can borrow
- the length of the mortgage
- how long you have to accept the offer
- about how much the closing costs will be

Closing

The final step is the closing. This is a meeting of the buyer, seller, lender, their lawyers, and others. At the closing, the buyer signs the loan papers and pays the closing costs. Closing costs include the down payment, less any deposit. They also include many taxes and fees. The taxes and fees can add thousands of dollars to closing costs.

At the end of the closing, you get the keys to your new home.

Chapter 12
Debt

Most people borrow money sometimes. Many of them are able to handle the debt. They repay their loans on time. They make more than the minimum payments on their credit cards.

But some people have too much debt. Why does this happen? Here are some common reasons:

- They lose their job.
- They get sick and can't work.
- Their household loses a wage earner through divorce or death.
- They need money for an emergency.
- They don't know how to manage their money.
- They buy more things than they can afford.

How much debt is too much for you? The activities on pages 64–65 help you consider this question. The self-test on page 64 looks at how you act and feel. Are your debts causing you problems?

Experts also use formulas to decide how much debt is too much. One common formula is this one. Mortgage lenders use it to decide if borrowers have too much debt.

Total	≤	36%
Total housing costs + debt payments	should be no more than	36% of your income (before taxes)

The activity on page 65 lets you apply this formula to your own finances.

Suppose you decide you have too much debt. Maybe you can't even pay all your bills. What can you do?

See Where You Stand

The first thing to do is take a close look at your spending plan. Chapters 2–4 give details on making a spending plan. Figure out your income and your expenses. Next, figure out how much you need to cut to get by.

Cut Expenses

You may be able to cut some expenses down to zero. For example, delay buying new clothes until your money problems are solved. Put off taking classes or joining clubs.

Here are other suggestions for cutting expenses during a crisis:

- Stop eating out. It is almost always cheaper to eat at home. If you are going to be away from home all day, pack a lunch.
- Use the car only for necessary trips. That will cut down on how much gas you use. It will also decrease wear and tear on the car. If possible, walk, take a bus, or share rides.
- If you have a VCR, rent a video rather than going to a movie. Renting a video costs only a few dollars, no matter how many people watch it.

- Invest time rather than money. If you can, shovel your own walk or mow your own lawn instead of paying someone else. Is someone in the family good at cutting hair? Maybe you can save the expense of haircuts.
- Agree that no big purchases will be made without discussing them first.

Groceries are one expense that can usually be cut down. Here are some tips.

- Make a shopping list and stick to it.
- Reduce the number of shopping trips you make each week. Try to get all of your groceries in one trip.
- Choose less costly cuts of meat. Make some meatless meals.
- Don't toss leftovers. Reheat them in a microwave.

See Chapter 5, page 24, for other smart shopping tips.

Too Much Debt? Warning Signs

How do you know if you have too much debt? Try this self-test.

True   False

____   ____   **1.** I don't know how much I owe.

____   ____   **2.** I pay only the minimum amounts each month.

____   ____   **3.** I often pay bills late.

____   ____   **4.** My total debt rarely shrinks.

____   ____   **5.** I often take money out of my savings to pay monthly bills.

____   ____   **6.** I can't pay all my bills each month, so I rotate payments.

____   ____   **7.** I've borrowed on one credit card to pay off another.

____   ____   **8.** I've taken out a new loan to pay old loans.

____   ____   **9.** I often use the line of credit on my checking account.

____   ____   **10.** I use credit for items that I used to buy with cash.

____   ____   **11.** I rely on overtime pay to make ends meet.

____   ____   **12.** More than 20 percent of my take-home pay goes for debt payments. (This doesn't include mortgage payments.)

____   ____   **13.** I spend more than I earn.

____   ____   **14.** I would have money problems right away if I lost my job.

____   ____   **15.** I often worry about how I will pay my bills.

____   ____   **16.** My debts are making my home life unhappy.

If you answered True to more than one or two questions, you could have a problem with debt.

How Much Do You Pay per Month?

Look at your level of debt by answering these questions.

1. What is your *yearly* household income before taxes? $ _____

2. What is your *monthly* household income before taxes? $ _____
(answer to item 1 ÷ 12)

3. What is 36% of your monthly household income? $ _____
(answer to item 2 × .36)

4. Total Housing Costs

    a. Monthly mortgage or rent payment $ _____

    b. Property taxes per month (if paid separately)   + _____

    c. Homeowner's or renter's insurance per month   + _____
      (if paid separately)

    Total monthly housing costs $ _____

5. Housing Costs + Debt Payments

    a. Total monthly housing costs (from item 4) $ _____

    b. Car payment   + _____

    c. Credit cards—total payments per month   + _____

    d. Installment purchase payments per month   + _____

    e. Bank loan or overdraft protection   + _____
      payments per month

    f. Other loans—payments per month   + _____

    g. Other debts—payments per month   + _____

    Total housing costs + debt payments $ _____

Is your total in item 5 more or less than your answer in item 3? If it's
more, you may have too much debt.

Contact Your Creditors

Suppose you've cut your spending as much as you can. What if you still can't pay all your bills? First, contact your creditors (the people or companies you owe money to).

☞ Don't just stop paying your bills. Your creditors will assume you don't intend to pay. They may hire a collection agency to get the money from you.

Tell your creditors that you intend to pay your bills. Let them know you're having problems. They may be willing to work something out. Most creditors would rather get a small payment than nothing at all. Negative information may still show up on your credit report. But doing something will look better than doing nothing.

You and your creditors may be able to agree on one of these approaches:

- You make smaller payments for a short time. Then you start making regular payments again.
- You refinance the loan. That means you sign a new loan contract. You will make smaller payments over a longer period of time.

☞ Refinancing reduces your monthly payments. But it may cost you more in the long run.

Get Credit Counseling

Maybe you've tried everything and still can't pay your bills. It may be time to speak to a credit counselor.

National Foundation for Consumer Credit member agencies, usually called Consumer Credit Counseling Service, provide credit counseling. It costs very little or nothing. Call (800) 388-2227 to find the nearest office.

Other options include the Better Business Bureau or a credit union in your area. Before you agree to counseling, find out what the fee is.

A credit counselor can

- review your income, expenses, and debts
- help you set up a spending plan
- help arrange reduced payments for you
- help you plan for future expenses
- suggest options you hadn't thought of

Bankruptcy

For serious money problems, bankruptcy may be the only solution. But it is a last resort.

Bankruptcy law is complex, and each person's money problems are different. This section gives some general information. But if you're thinking about bankruptcy, you need more facts than this book can present. Your best bet is to talk with a lawyer. Try to find one who is an expert in bankruptcy law.

If you're deeply in debt, bankruptcy has some advantages. But it also has some serious drawbacks. The chart below sums up some of the important ones.

If you file for bankruptcy, it can affect your financial future for years. You may have trouble getting credit again. You could also have trouble getting a job or renting an apartment.

If You're Deep in Debt	
Advantages of Bankruptcy	**Drawbacks of Bankruptcy**
• It wipes out most of your debts. • If you own your home, you may not lose it. • Your creditors can't sue or harass you. (They may file objections to your bankruptcy, though.) • It gives you a chance to start again.	• You have to go to a legal hearing. • You lose some privacy. In some cases, you lose control of your own money. • It may damage your credit. (Bankruptcy can stay on your credit history for up to 10 years.) • You still must pay some debts. • Some people feel bankruptcy is shameful.

Chapter 13

Insurance

When you buy insurance, you agree to pay a premium. This is a set amount that you pay regularly. The insurance company agrees to pay you benefits. An insurance contract spells out when you get benefits.

Experts suggest five kinds of insurance:

- health insurance
- homeowner's or renter's insurance
- car insurance
- disability insurance
- life insurance

Health Insurance

Health insurance helps pay for health care. Some kinds pay only if you're sick. Others pay for care to prevent illness, such as checkups.

Group policies have lower premiums than individual policies. Many people get group health insurance through their employer. You may also be able to buy group health insurance through other groups.

Some people buy individual policies on their own. This is costly, but experts say it's worth the money. Without insurance, a long illness or a hospital stay could cost everything you have.

Government programs provide some health insurance for certain groups. Medicare covers some care for people over 65. Medicaid covers care for people with low incomes. These programs don't cover everything, though. Some states have programs that help you get health insurance for your children.

Homeowner's Insurance

Homeowner's insurance helps fix damage to your house. It may also help pay if someone is hurt on your property and sues you. Many policies also cover the contents of your home. You get money to replace them if they are stolen or damaged. (Note: You may have to buy a separate policy to get this coverage.) Experts say you should insure your house for at least 80 percent of the replacement value. The replacement value is what it would cost to rebuild the house, which may be more than you paid for it. You can also choose to insure a house for its full replacement value.

Many homeowner's policies have a high deductible—sometimes thousands of dollars. This is the amount of a loss that you would have to pay. The insurance would cover amounts over that.

You can get homeowner's insurance for a condo or co-op apartment.

Renter's Insurance

If you rent, renter's insurance protects the contents of your home. It will pay if your possessions are stolen or destroyed.

Car Insurance

After a car accident, car insurance helps pay for the damage.

If you're found to be at fault, your insurance will pay any medical bills. It will also pay to fix any damage you caused. This is called liability coverage.

Car insurance can also pay you if your car is stolen, vandalized, or damaged by weather. This is called comprehensive coverage.

In many states, you must have car insurance. If you drive without it, you can lose your driver's license or vehicle registration.

Disability Insurance

If you're sick or hurt and can't work for a long time, you lose income. Disability insurance can help pay your living expenses.

Check with your employer or human resources department. Find out what kind of disability coverage you can get.

Life Insurance

When you buy life insurance, you name one or more beneficiaries. The insurance company will pay these people when you die.

How much life insurance should you have? It depends on what you want it to do. Pay for your funeral? Pay off your mortgage? Send your kids to college? Support your family?

Your employer may offer life insurance. If not, or if you need more, you can buy your own.

Don't waste your money on life insurance for kids. Children don't need life insurance.

Things to Consider

About Health Insurance
- How much are the premiums?
- Is there a deductible? A co-payment? How much will you pay when you go for treatment?
- What does the policy cover? Does it meet your needs? Does it include coverage you don't need?
- How do you make a claim? How easy or hard is it?
- Can you choose your own health care providers?

About Homeowner's or Renter's Insurance
- How much are the premiums?
- What is the deductible?
- What kind of damage does it cover? Is any damage not covered?
- How does it pay a claim? Do you have to fix the damage first? Or does it pay you first?
- How much will it pay for the contents of your home?
- Homeowner's: How much will it pay if your home is destroyed?

About Car Insurance
- How much are the premiums?
- What is the deductible?
- What kinds of losses does it cover? How much will it pay for each?

About Disability Insurance
- How much are the premiums?
- How long will coverage last?
- What disabilities qualify for benefits?
- How long must you be disabled before you get benefits?
- How much will the insurance pay if you're disabled?
- How long will the payments last?
- If you die while disabled, will your survivors get any benefits?

About Life Insurance
- How much are the premiums? Will they increase over time?
- How much will the insurance pay your survivors? Is that enough for their needs?
- How long will coverage last? For a certain number of years? For the rest of your life?

Match each insurance term with its definition. Then answer the questions about your insurance policies.

_____	**1.** premium
_____	**2.** group policy
_____	**3.** benefits
_____	**4.** replacement value
_____	**5.** disability
_____	**6.** liability coverage
_____	**7.** deductible
_____	**8.** beneficiary
_____	**9.** comprehensive coverage
_____	**10.** co-payment

a. the amount of a loss you pay before your insurance pays anything

b. the amount you pay each year for an insurance policy

c. the person paid by your life insurance when you die

d. insurance that pays if your car is damaged by weather or stolen

e. a policy you get through your job or an organization

f. the amount an insurance policy pays

g. a physical or mental condition that prevents you from working

h. the amount you pay when you get medical care or drugs

i. insurance that pays if you are at fault in a car accident

j. the amount of money needed to replace a home

Answers on page 80.

- What insurance policies do you have?

_____

- If you have health, homeowner's or renter's, or car insurance, what is the deductible for each policy?

_____

- If you have life insurance, who is the beneficiary?

_____

Chapter 14

Investing

Investing means putting your money where you think it will earn more money. Experts say you should have a sound financial base before you start investing. A sound financial base includes

- three to six months' income in savings and/or CDs for emergencies
- life, health, and property insurance
- home ownership, if that is one of your goals

You might also want to have a retirement plan before you invest. Or that might be a goal of your investments.

Once you have a sound financial base, you can decide what to do with your remaining money.

This chapter covers some of the basics of investments. But investing is a complex process. Before you invest, you may want to get some advice. Some places to look are

- financial magazines and newspapers
- TV or radio shows on money management and investing
- stock brokers, insurance agents, and financial planners

☞

Financial planners may charge a fee. Or they may get a commission on certain investments they sell. If they work for commissions, they may try harder to sell you those investments. If they work for a fee, they may present more options.

Types of Investments

With some investments, you loan your money. These investments include bonds and annuities. You hope to get a return for the use of your money. In some cases, you are guaranteed a return. With other investments, you buy something. You hope that the price will rise and you can sell it for a profit. These investments include real estate and stocks.

Investments range from very safe to very risky. If you put your money into a low-risk investment, there is very little chance you will lose it. But your profits will probably be lower. If you put your money into a high-risk investment, the chance of losing part or all of it is greater. But the chance of making a lot of money is greater too.

Most people choose several different investments. They put some money in safer investments with lower returns. And they put some money in riskier investments with the chance of higher returns. This lets them keep some money safe and earn good profits, too.

The table below describes some common investments.

Savings Bonds	<ul><li>Issued by U.S. government.</li><li>Sold at most banks.</li><li>Don't require a lot of money.</li><li>No risk.</li></ul>
Annuities	<ul><li>Investor buys with lump sum payment.</li><li>Annuity pays you regularly in the future.</li><li>Most often pays off during retirement.</li><li>Often nontaxable until payments begin.</li><li>Low risk.</li></ul>
Mutual Funds	<ul><li>Fund is groups of stocks, bonds, and other investments managed by investment experts.</li><li>Each investor buys shares in the fund.</li><li>Fund regularly pays profits to investors.</li><li>Investors can sell shares to make a profit, but may lose money if value has decreased.</li><li>Levels of risk and return vary.</li></ul>
Bonds	<ul><li>Investor loans money to government or corporation that issues the bond.</li><li>Bonds take 5 to 20 years to mature.</li><li>Low to moderate risk.</li></ul>
Stocks	<ul><li>Investor buys shares of ownership in corporation.</li><li>Stocks rise in value when corporation does well. Stocks may decrease in value.</li><li>Success requires knowledge of the stock market.</li><li>Risk varies.</li></ul>
Real Estate	<ul><li>Investor may make money by buying property and renting it out.</li><li>Investor may make money by buying property and selling it for a profit.</li><li>Moderate to high risk.</li></ul>

Saving for Retirement

You can put your retirement savings in any kind of investment. But several plans are designed specifically for retirement savings.

Some retirement investments are safer than others. Think carefully about how to invest your money. Should you keep it where you know it will be safe? Or can you take a risk for higher earnings? Do you want a number of investments with different levels of risk?

Retirement Plans	<ul><li>In some retirement plans, your employer makes contributions in your name.</li><li>In other retirement plans, you contribute to a company plan.</li><li>The plan invests the money.</li><li>When you retire, the plan pays you.</li><li>You may get regular payments over time. Or you may get one lump sum.</li></ul>
Social Security	<ul><li>While you're working, the government withholds Social Security tax from your paycheck. Your employer also makes a contribution for you.</li><li>You can collect full benefits when you turn 65. (The age will increase to 66 in 2009 and 67 in 2027.)</li><li>You can collect partial benefits if you retire at 62.</li><li>When you die, your spouse can collect benefits.</li><li>If you're divorced, you may be able to collect on your ex-spouse's Social Security. You must have been married for 10 years.</li><li>Experts say that Social Security should be only part of your retirement planning. By themselves, Social Security benefits won't allow you to live comfortably.</li></ul>

The best answers to these questions are not simple to find. They can depend on

- how close you are to retirement
- how much money you make
- how much money you'll need
- what other expenses you have
- how much you've saved already
- your feelings about different investments
- your comfort with different levels of risk

An expert can help you pick the best approach for you.

IRAs (Individual Retirement Accounts)	• IRAs are special accounts with banks, brokerages, or mutual funds. They help you save for retirement. • You can save a percentage of your income. • You can choose where your money is invested. • With regular IRAs, you don't pay taxes on the money until you retire. • With Roth IRAs, you pay taxes on the money you deposit. But whatever the investment earns is tax-free. • If you withdraw money before you're 59½, you have to pay a penalty.
401(k) or 403(b) Plans	• These are special accounts set up by your company. • You can put a percentage of your income in the account. Your company will often match your contribution. • You can have your contribution taken right out of your paycheck. • If you withdraw money before retirement, you may have to pay a penalty. • You don't have to pay taxes on the contributions or the interest until you begin withdrawing money. • The plan usually offers several investment options with varying levels of risk. You can choose which ones to put your money in.

Saving for Education

Many people invest to save for education. They may invest long-term to send their kids to college. Or they may invest short-term to go back to school themselves.

Many people use these investments to save for school:
- CDs
- U.S. savings bonds
- mutual funds
- bonds
- Education IRAs (special accounts that let you save for education. The earnings are tax-free.)
- other special education savings plans set up by federal or state law

Suppose you decide to use investments to pay school costs. Experts say these ideas will help:

- Start early (if investing long-term).
- Add regularly (if investing long-term).
- Time your investments. Make sure they will pay off when you need the money.
- Consider income tax. Tax-free investments may leave you more money to spend. But they may also earn less than taxable investments. Profits from some municipal bonds are tax-free. Interest on U.S. savings bonds is tax-free if used to pay for school. (You must meet income requirements.)
- Think carefully about risk. More risk may mean more profits. But it could also mean losing your money.

The closer you are to needing the money, the safer your investments should be.

Now that you have read *Control Your Money,* list 10 changes you want to make in the way you control your money.

Examples:

• My family and I will write down everything we spend for the next four weeks. We will use the results in making a household spending plan.

• I will keep a file of all my deposit and withdrawal slips and ATM receipts. I will check them against my monthly bank statement.

• I will use only one credit card. I will close out my other credit card accounts.

_____

_____

_____

_____

_____

_____

_____

_____

_____

_____

_____

_____

_____

_____

Chapter 15
For More Information

Consumer Contacts

AARP
Web site: http://www.aarp.org/money/consumer

Better Business Bureau
To locate the Better Business Bureau nearest you, contact the
Council of Better Business Bureaus, Inc.
Address: 4200 Wilson Blvd.
         Arlington, VA 22203
Phone: (703) 525-8277
Web site: http://www.bbb.org/

Consumer Federation of America
Address: 1424 16th Street, NW
         Suite 604
         Washington, DC 20036
Phone: (202) 387-6121
Web site: http://www.consumerfed.org/

Consumer's Resource Handbook
Available from the Consumer Information Center
Phone: (888) 8PUEBLO
E-mail: catalog.pueblo@gsa.gov
Web site: http://www.pueblo.gsa.gov/
Lists consumer contacts in government, business, and nonprofits

Consumers Union
Address: 101 Truman Ave.
         Yonkers, NY 10703-1057
Phone: (914) 378-2000
Web site: http://www.consumersunion.org/

Federal Trade Commission
Address: CRC-240
Washington, DC 20580
Phone: (877) FTC-HELP
Web site: http://www.ftc.gov/bcp/consumer.shtm

Social Security

Social Security Administration
Phone: (800) 772-1213
Web site: http://www.ssa.gov/

Credit Reports

To check your credit report, send your request to three credit reporting agencies: Experian, Trans Union, and Equifax. Or go to http://www.annualcreditreport.com.

Experian
Address: Experian National Consumer Assistance Center
PO Box 2104
Allen, TX 75013-2104
Phone: (888) EXPERIAN
Web site: http://www.experian.com

Trans Union
Address: Trans Union LLC
Consumer Disclosure Center
PO Box 390
Springfield, PA 19064-0390
Phone: (800) 888-4213
Web site: http://www.transunion.com/corporate/personal/personal.page

Equifax
Address: CSC Credit Services or CBI Credit Services
Customer Assistance Center
PO Box 105873
Atlanta, GA 30348
Phone: (800) 685-1111 (to order a credit report)
Web site: http://www.equifax.com

Credit Counseling

National Foundation for Consumer Credit, Inc.
Use one of these sources to find the office nearest you:
Phone: (800) 388-2227 (24-hour automated line)
    (800) 682-9832 (Spanish language line, available weekdays
    9:00–5:00 Eastern time)
E-mail: info@nfcc.org
Web site: http://www.nfcc.org/financialeducation/consumertools.cfm

Insurance

National Insurance Consumer Helpline
Phone: (800) 942-4242

Federal Income Tax

Internal Revenue Service
Phone: (800) 829-1040 (assistance line)
Web site: http://www.irs.ustreas.gov/

Answer Key

Review Checking Terms (p. 38)

1. d	6. e
2. g	7. j
3. i	8. c
4. h	9. b
5. a	10. f

Reading a Credit Report (p. 52)

1. VISA, Sears, Chase
2. Chase; VISA
3. $245; $9,762
4. Sears; $635
5. September 1997
6. 4

7. Credit Reporting
   321 Main St. Suite 17
   Springfield, MA 01101

Know Your Credit Card (p. 57)

1. c	5. a
2. e	6. h
3. f	7. d
4. g	8. b

Understand Your Insurance (p. 71)

1. b	6. i
2. e	7. a
3. f	8. c
4. j	9. d
5. g	10. h